SACRED SKIES

— ✦ The facts and the fables ✦ —

 ✦

Finn Bevan
Illustrated by Diana Mayo

CHILDREN'S PRESS®
A Division of Grolier Publishing
LONDON • NEW YORK • HONG KONG • SYDNEY
DANBURY, CONNECTICUT

First American Edition by
Children's Press
A Division of Grolier Publishing Co., Inc.
Sherman Turnpike
Danbury, Connecticut 06813

Series editor: Rachel Cooke
Art director: Robert Walster
Designer: Mo Choy
Picture research: Sue Mennell

A CIP catalog record for this book is available from the Library of Congress.

Printed in Singapore

Picture acknowledgments:
Bruce Coleman p. 6 (Dr. Scott Nielsen);
E.T. Archive p. 17 (British Museum); **Eye Ubiquitous** p.13 (P. M. Field);
Werner Forman Archive pp. 12b (National Museum of Anthropology, Mexico),
27 (Statens Historiska Museum, Stockholm);
Robert Harding Picture Library pp. 20, 22, 26;
The Image Bank 12t, 16; **Panos Pictures** p. 7 (Jim Holmes);
UCLA Fowler Museum of Cultural History (Gift of Jerome L. Joss) p.23

Contents

✦

The Skies Above

From ancient times, people have held the skies in awe. The power of a thunderstorm, the beauty of the Moon and stars, the dazzling light of the Sun—all were crucial for life on Earth. As a result, people worshipped them all as gods or spirits, whose actions caused day and night, the changing seasons, and the weather. Their deeds were told in myths and legends, seeking to explain and make sense of the sacred skies.

Sacred Skies

People used the Sun, the Moon, and stars as natural timekeepers long before the invention of clocks. They were also used for navigation long before compasses and charts. But because people did not understand the scientific reasons for the movements of the heavenly bodies, the changing seasons, and sunrise and sunset, they believed they were controlled by the gods.

The gods who controlled the Sun and the Moon were the most influential. An eclipse of the Sun was interpreted as the Sun going out—the most terrible omen of disaster. The gods of the weather were awesome, too. A storm could easily ruin crops, as well as bringing life-giving rain.

In many cultures, the sky itself was worshipped as a god or goddess. The ancient Egyptian sky goddess was Nut. She was held in an arc above Earth by Shu, the god of air. The world itself was created by the great Sun god, Re. The skies were also believed to be the home of the gods, a heavenly place from which they controlled events on Earth.

Ancient astronomers were skilled observers of the skies. This made them very powerful. People believed that their destinies were controlled by the movements of the Moon and stars. They consulted the astronomers to tell them their future.

Spirits of the Sun

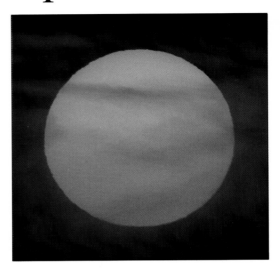

The Sun is a star—a huge ball of burning gases—which lies at the center of our solar system. Around the Sun circle nine planets, among them Earth, which takes a year to complete its orbit around the Sun. Although 100 million miles from Earth, the Sun is vital for life on this planet, but, in fact, it is just one of millions of stars in the universe.

Life-giving Heat

Without the Sun's heat and light, nothing could live or grow on Earth. Small wonder then that ancient peoples considered the Sun the most powerful god in the sky. They worshipped it, built temples to honor it, and told many stories to explain its daily rising and setting.

How the Sun Came to Be

According to a myth from the South Pacific, there was once only the Moon and stars but no Sun. Then a man quarreled with the emu, his friend, and stole one of the eggs from its nest. He threw the egg into the sky. There it hit a pile of firewood, which immediately burst into flames. And this is how the Sun came to be.

Spirits of the Earth

The ancient religion of Japan is called Shinto, which means the "way of the gods." Its followers believe in spirits, called *kami*, which live in natural places, such as mountains, trees, paddy fields, and rivers. People leave offerings at these sacred places, such as those pictured here tied to an ancient tree. The Sun, the Moon, and stars are also homes to *kami*, and the most important *kami* of all is Amaterasu, goddess of the Sun. She is worshipped both as a goddess and as the ancestor of the emperors of Japan. There are many stories about her adventures.

The Day the Sun Went Out

This is a Shinto story of how Amaterasu quarreled with her brother and took the Sun out of the sky.

◆

Susano, the storm god, was furious. He ranted and raged and howled and wept. In fact, he behaved so badly that his father could stand it no longer. He banished his son to the underworld, never to darken Earth again. Before he left, Susano begged a favor, to say good-bye to his sister, the Sun goddess, Amaterasu. His wish was granted.

Susano set off for the sacred hall where his sister and her maids were weaving the clothes of the gods. But his departure caused a violent earthquake and made Amaterasu suspect that her brother's arrival meant trouble. She prepared herself for battle, with a quiverful of arrows and a mighty bow.

"Don't worry, sister," Susano said. "I've only come to say good-bye, not to harm you."

"Prove it," the Sun goddess replied.

And she challenged him to a contest. If he could somehow beat her in producing five strong sons, she would believe him.

So the contest began. The Sun goddess took her brother's sword and broke it into three pieces. She crunched these up and spat them out, as three graceful daughters. Then Susano took his sister's necklace and chewed the jewels in his mouth. Then he breathed out, and from his breath came five strong sons. The storm god had won.

But Amaterasu was not happy.

"The jewels came from my necklace," she said. "And so, by rights, I am the winner!"

"What?" snorted her brother. "I won, fair and square!"

And they began to quarrel. Susano grew angrier and angrier. He'd won, he shouted. She was just a bad loser, he screamed. Then, in a furious fit of temper, he picked up his horse and hurled it through the roof of the weaving hall, causing mayhem and chaos inside.

Amaterasu fled in terror and went to hide in a cave. And as she hid, the world was plunged into darkness. The rice fields lay barren and nothing would grow. In desperation, the eight hundred gods of heaven met together to decide how to coax Amaterasu out again.

One of the wisest gods, Omorikane, was given the problem to solve. After a great deal of thought, he hatched a cunning plot. One god made a long rope of jewels. Another made a magical mirror. They hung these from the branches of a sacred tree, which they planted outside the cave.

Then the beautiful goddess of the dawn climbed on top of an upturned tub and began to dance for all she was worth. She twisted and turned and clowned around so much that the eight hundred gods roared with laughter.

The sound reached Amaterasu hiding in her cave and made her very curious. She opened the door just the tiniest crack and called out: "Why are you laughing?" she asked. "And why are you dancing like that?"

" We're rejoicing," the goddess of the dawn replied, "because we've found a goddess even greater than you. Look."

While she was speaking, two gods pointed the mirror at the cave door while another hid nearby. When Amaterasu caught sight of her reflection, she slowly came out of the cave to get a better look. Suddenly, the hidden god grabbed her hand and pulled her out. The rope of jewels was stretched across the cave, to stop her going back inside.

After this, things quickly got back to normal. The Sun shone again and light returned to the world. There was just one task left—to punish the wicked Susano, who had started all the trouble. The eight hundred gods cut off his beard and his fingernails and toenails, and banished him from heaven, once and for all.

Phases of the Moon

At a distance of 239,000 miles, the Moon is Earth's closest neighbor in space. The Moon orbits Earth once every 27 days—approximately a month. As it moves, it seems to change shape from a thin sliver to a round, full Moon and back again. This is because, on its journey, different amounts of the Moon are lit by the Sun. The Moon gives off no light of its own.

Moon Months

Throughout the centuries, people have gazed at the Moon, worshipped it, and studied its changing face. For ancient people, the changes in the Moon marked the passing months. They used this knowledge and their knowledge of the Sun to draw up the first calendars. The Moon was also a powerful god or goddess, often the partner, sister, or brother of the Sun.

An Aztec calenda stone. The Aztec calendar wa based on the movement of the Sur and the Moon

Changing Face

The changes in the Moon's shape are called phases. There are many myths to explain them. In Africa, they are said to go back to a time long ago when the Moon boasted that it was more beautiful than the Sun. Furious, the Sun broke the Moon into pieces. Since then, the Moon has been so scared of the Sun, it only rarely dares to show its whole face in the night sky.

Chinese Moons

In Chinese mythology, the Moon's full, round shape is a symbol of family unity. During the Festival of the Moon, held at the time of the autumn full Moon, people sit up to view the Moon and write poems and songs in its praise. In the evening, a great feast is held. Special Moon-shaped cakes, like those being made in the photograph, are eaten during the festival.

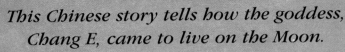

Lady in the Moon

This Chinese story tells how the goddess, Chang E, came to live on the Moon.

◆

There was once a beautiful goddess, named Chang E. She lived in heaven with her husband, Yi, the archer. At that time there were ten Suns, not one, which were meant to appear one by one in the sky. One day, without warning, all ten appeared together, and Earth was scorched by their fearsome heat.

The Lord of Heaven sent for Yi. He told him to go down to Earth, to frighten the Suns and bring them under control. So Yi took his bow and a quiver of arrows, and he and his wife descended to Earth. But the sight of the people and their terrible suffering made him so angry, he shot the Suns and killed them, until only one was left in the sky.

The Lord of Heaven was furious. He condemned Yi and Chang E to live on Earth as mortals, not gods. In despair, Yi searched for the elixir of everlasting life.

At last, he found what he was looking for, but there was a catch: "Here is enough elixir for two," he was told. "But woe betide if one person drinks it all. He or she will leave the world and never return."

Chang E longed to go back to heaven and her happy, carefree life. She stole the elixir and drank it all down, regardless of the warning. And woe betide her indeed! Off she floated to the Moon, where she turned from a goddess into a toad, her only companions a hare and an old, old man, chopping wood.

When Yi discovered his wife's betrayal, he was full of dismay. Would he never become a god again? But the Lord of Heaven took pity on him. Yi was allowed to return to heaven, while the foolish Chang E was changed back into a beautiful goddess and allowed to live in the Palace of the Moon, where Yi could go and visit her.

Seeing Stars

There are millions of stars in the sky, formed from huge clouds of gases. Inside the stars, the gases react together, creating intense heat and light. A night sky full of sparkling stars inspired many ancient myths and legends, as well as the belief that the stars held the key to foreseeing the future.

Stargazers

Among the Navaho people of North America, a stargazer is called if someone falls ill. He examines his patient, then walks into the night. He chants and prays to the star spirits, then raises a crystal to the brightest star. Gazing deep inside, he sees the cause of the illness and so can then cure it.

Aquarius

Aries

Pisces

Gemini

Taurus

Cancer

Greek Astronomers

The ancient Greeks were great astronomers, who made many discoveries by studying the stars. One astronomer, Hipparchus, located 850 stars long before anyone else. The Greeks saw that many of the stars formed patterns, or constellations, in the sky. They named many constellations after the heroes and gods they worshipped. We still use these names today.

Signs of the Zodiac

Around 400 B.C., the Greeks identified a band of stars through which the Sun appeared to move throughout the year. They called it the zodiac. It was made up of twelve constellations—the twelve signs of the zodiac. Many of the signs were named after animals, such as Pisces, the fish, and Taurus, the bull. These names were already very ancient and may have been used by the Sumerians, who lived in the Middle East around 3000 B.C.

Leo

Scorpio

Sagittarius

Virgo

Libra

Capricorn

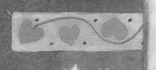

The Hunter in the Sky

*This is a story from ancient Greece about how Orion,
the hunter, took his place in the sky.*

One of the most famous constellations in the
sky is that of Orion, the hunter. Look for him when
night next falls. Orion was once a mighty hunter, handsome and
brave. He was also a giant, tall and strong, with the power to walk
through the sea. Wherever he went, his faithful dog, Sirius, followed.
Artemis, the beautiful goddess of the Moon, fell madly in love with
Orion and invited him to Crete to go hunting. There was just one problem—
her brother, Apollo, hated the giant and vowed to kill him if he could.
At first, all went well. But soon Orion began to boast that he was strong
enough to kill all the wild animals on Crete. Earth goddess, Gaea, heard his
boast and sent a scorpion to sting the hunter and teach him a lesson.
Orion fought bravely, but even he could not kill the scorpion.
Instead, he dived into the sea and began to walk through the
water toward a nearby island.

Waiting on the island was Artemis—and so
was Apollo, plotting a trick to play on his sister.
Knowing full well that it must be Orion, he bet his sister that
she could not hit a dark, distant shape among the waves. Artemis
took aim and fired her arrow, which hit Orion and killed him.
When Artemis realized what she had done, she was full of sorrow.
She begged the gods to bring Orion back to life, but they would not grant
her wish. So she placed Orion in the sky among the stars, where he
could shine forever, sword in hand, followed by his faithful dog. The
constellation of Scorpio, the scorpion, is behind them—Orion is
doomed to flee forever from its stinging tail.

Life-giving Rain

Raindrops form from tiny water droplets inside clouds or from melting crystals of ice. For a raindrop to fall, a thousand or more droplets must join together. Rain is essential for life on Earth. It makes the plants we eat grow and gives us water to drink. Because of this, the gods of rain were all-important to the people who worshipped them.

Aztec Weather Gods

The Aztecs of Central America worshipped many gods, among them the gods of the Sun, wind, and rain. Each day, the Sun god, Huitzilopochtli, battled against the forces of darkness. Ehecatl, the wind god, blew out the wind. But without Tlaloc, the mighty god of rain, the Sun and wind were worthless, for the rain made the Aztecs' corn grow. If no rain fell, famine would surely follow.

Lord of the Rains

*This is a story about Tlaloc,
the Aztec god of rain.*

Long ago, the mighty Tlaloc, god of rain, looked down on the world from his home in heaven. There he lived, surrounded by food, water, and beautiful flowers. The goddesses of corn also lived there, as did the god's helpers, the Tlaloques. Their laughter and songs rang out through the air.

Down on Earth, life was full of suffering. The land was dry and parched, and nothing would grow. People were hungry and in despair. Tlaloc saw all this from heaven and pledged his help.

The goggle-eyed god summoned his helpers, and together they climbed to the top of a high mountain. He put on his headdress of heron feathers. In one hand he took his lightning-bolt wand and held his thunder rattle in the other. "Bring the great jars," he boomed to the Tlaloques.

So the Tlaloques brought the four great jars—the first full of frost, the second of disease, the third of drought, and the fourth of rain.

Tlaloc picked up the fourth jar and smashed it down on the mountainside. The sky grew dark, a howling wind blew, thunder and lightning crashed through the sky. And then the rain fell down on Earth and brought the dry land back to life.

Arches in the Sky

Rainbows occur when the Sun comes out in wet weather: before, during, or after rain. The sunlight hits the raindrops and breaks up into seven colors—red, orange, yellow, green, blue, indigo, and violet. Red is always at the top of the rainbow's arch; violet is at the bottom. To see a rainbow, you must have your back to the Sun.

Chasing Rainbows

A brilliant rainbow arched across the sky is a magical sight in nature. Many myths have been told to explain it. In some, it is welcomed as a herald of rain. In others, it is a protective spirit, signaling the end of a violent storm. A pot of gold is said to lie at the end of a rainbow, a place that, sadly, you can never reach.

African Myths

Some African myths describe
the rainbow as a gigantic snake,
whose brilliant body encircles the
world and unites all the places on
Earth. In other stories, the rainbow is
seen as two snakes meeting in the sky.
Their arched bodies protect the land from
much feared thunderstorms.

A shrine sculpture from Nigeria.
Two "rainbow" snakes form an arch
over the human figure, while above
a leopard pounces on an antelope.

The Rainbow Serpent

The Aborigines of Australia believe that
the rainbow is a great serpent that lives
underground, guarding the water holes. When
it needs to move to a new water hole, it appears
as a rainbow in the sky. The rainbow serpent
brings life-giving rain, but, if angry, whips up
terrible storms and floods.

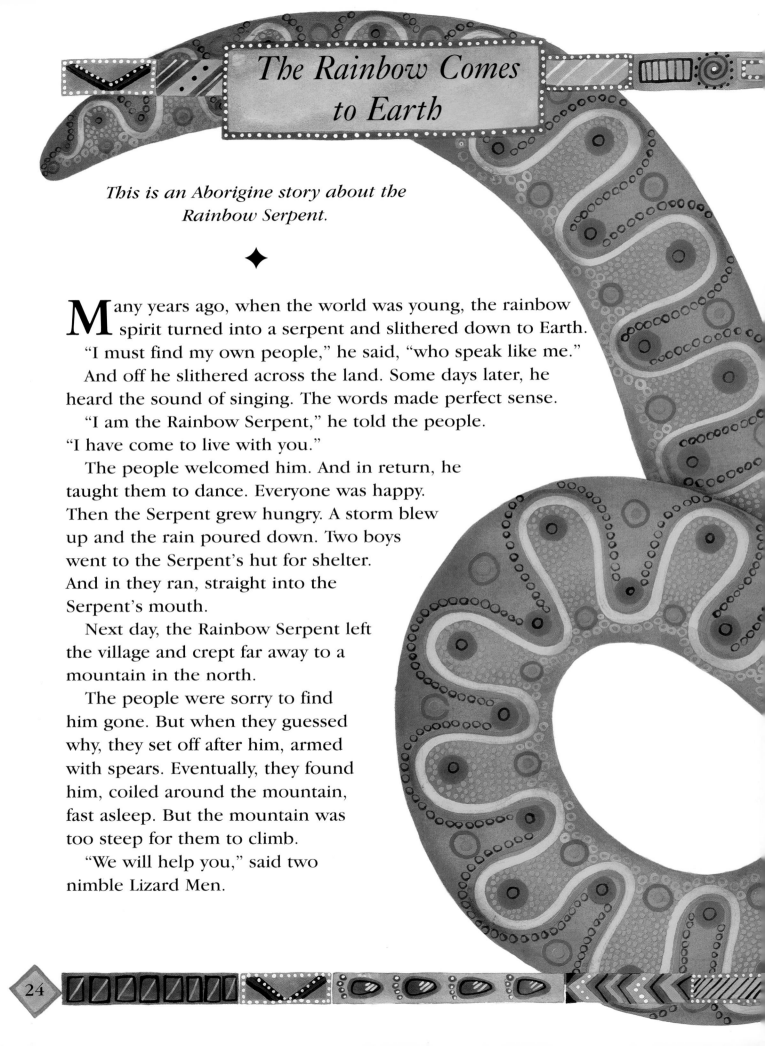

The Rainbow Comes to Earth

This is an Aborigine story about the Rainbow Serpent.

✦

Many years ago, when the world was young, the rainbow spirit turned into a serpent and slithered down to Earth.

"I must find my own people," he said, "who speak like me."

And off he slithered across the land. Some days later, he heard the sound of singing. The words made perfect sense.

"I am the Rainbow Serpent," he told the people. "I have come to live with you."

The people welcomed him. And in return, he taught them to dance. Everyone was happy. Then the Serpent grew hungry. A storm blew up and the rain poured down. Two boys went to the Serpent's hut for shelter. And in they ran, straight into the Serpent's mouth.

Next day, the Rainbow Serpent left the village and crept far away to a mountain in the north.

The people were sorry to find him gone. But when they guessed why, they set off after him, armed with spears. Eventually, they found him, coiled around the mountain, fast asleep. But the mountain was too steep for them to climb.

"We will help you," said two nimble Lizard Men.

Up the mountain they scrambled and cut a slit in the Serpent's side. There were no boys. Instead, two parrots flew out—all the colors of the rainbow—and off they soared. The people cheered as the Lizard Men returned. Then they heard a terrible sound. The Rainbow Serpent was stirring.

When the Serpent saw the hole in his side, he was very, very angry. He swished his tail from side to side and flicked his forked tongue. He smashed the mountain into pieces and sent them flying.

The terrified people ran away while thunder and lightning filled the sky, and torrents of rain poured down. Then hot and tired, the Rainbow Serpent slithered underground, where he lives to this day. Though sometimes he still leaps into the sky and arches his body over Earth, to see what people are doing.

Stirring-up Storms

Lightning is a giant spark of electricity released from a thundercloud. It races from the cloud to the ground, and back again. As it streaks along, it can heat the air in its path to a staggering 54,000 °F. The heated air expands at great speed, causing the booming noise we know as thunder. You see lightning before you hear thunder, even though both are made at exactly the same time. This is because light travels faster than sound.

Angry Gods

In ancient times, thunder and lightning were greatly feared, for they meant that the gods were angry. Thunder was thought to be the sound of the gods roaring with rage; lightning was their weapons hurled from the heavens. In Greek myth, Zeus, the king of the gods, ruled over gods and people alike armed with his mighty thunderbolt.

Myths of the North

The Norsemen, or Vikings, were seafaring warriors from Scandinavia. War played a large part in their lives and this is reflected in their myths, as well as the harsh northern weather they endured. Many tales were told of battles between the gods, the forces of good, and the evil frost giants. For the gods stood for law, order, and prosperity, which the frost giants were constantly trying to destroy.

Thor, the Thunderer

One of the most important Norse gods was Thor, the thunder god. He was extremely strong and had a temper to match. His famous weapon was the hammer, Mjöllnir, the "Destroyer," which he used to kill giants. Mjöllnir's ringing blows caused thunder and lightning. The Viking amulet above is shaped like Mjöllnir. It was worn as a lucky charm.

Thor's Lost Hammer

*This Viking story tells how Mjöllnir
was stolen and found again.*

One morning in Asgard, home of the gods,
Thor woke to find Mjöllnir missing.

"Oh, where is my hammer? Where is it?"
he ranted and raged. "How will I fight
the giants without it?"

The gods were worried. They held a
council to decide what to do.

"I'll go and find it," said the mischievous god,
Loki. He turned into a falcon and off he flew far and
wide in search of it. At last he came back with news. The
frost giant, Thrym, had stolen the hammer and
would give it back, but on one condition—that Freyja,
the goddess of love, would be his bride.

When she heard this, Freyja wept so hard that
her tears turned to gold, and the gods took pity on her
plight. Heimdall, the watchman, came up with a plan.
"Let's dress Thor in a wedding dress and veil and send
him as Freyja instead," he said. "He can take Loki
along as a bridesmaid!"

Thor was not very happy when he heard the plan.
But if it meant getting Mjöllnir back, he had to
agree. So he and Loki set off.

When they arrived at the giant's great hall,
Thrym was waiting to greet them. Inside the
hall, a great wedding feast was laid out for
the guests.

"Come in, come in, my pretty
one," cooed Thrym. "Eat,
drink, and make merry."

Through his veil, Thor's eyes lit up and he soon set to work on the food and drink. Thrym was surprised at his bride's enormous appetite: she ate one whole ox and eight large salmon and drank not one but three barrels of mead. Quick-thinking Loki explained it by saying that, in the excitement, she hadn't eaten for days.

At last came the moment to bless the bride. Mjöllnir was brought in and laid in her lap, as custom decreed. Thor had his chance. He grabbed the hammer and threw off his veil. While Thrym gasped in amazement, Thor struck him to the ground. Then Thor returned to Asgard in triumph, with Mjöllnir held firmly in his hand.

Notes and Explanations

Who's Who

ABORIGINES: The original inhabitants of Australia. The Aborigines traditionally lived as nomadic hunter-gatherers. To them, the natural world is sacred, created long ago during the Dreamtime. Since the arrival of European settlers, however, the Aborigines have struggled to keep their culture alive.

ANCIENT EGYPTIANS: The people who lived in Egypt from about 5000-30 B.C. They worshipped many gods and goddesses who controlled the natural world and daily life.

ANCIENT GREEKS: The people who lived in Greece from about 2000-30 B.C. Myths formed an important part of their religion and were used to explain the natural world and the exploits of the gods and heroes.

AZTECS: From the 13th to the early 16th centuries, the Aztecs ruled an empire that covered much of Mexico. Their civilization was destroyed by Spanish invaders. Their gods included the wind, rain, and the Sun, to whom they sacrificed human hearts and blood.

NAVAHO: A group of native North Americans who live in the southwest U.S. They have an elaborate system of myths and ceremonies.

SHINTO: The ancient religion of Japan, known as the "way of the spirits." Its followers worship spirits, called *kami*, which live in sacred places in the natural world.

SUMERIANS: The Sumerians lived in the area of modern Iraq some 5,000 years ago. They invented the first system of writing.

VIKINGS: The Vikings were a seafaring people from Scandinavia who raided and conquered many parts of northern Europe between the 8th and 11th centuries A.D.

What's What

Strictly speaking, fables, legends, and myths are all slightly different. But the three terms are often used to mean the same thing—a symbolic story or a story with a message.

FABLE: A short story, not based on fact, which often has animals as its central characters and a strong moral lesson to teach.

LEGEND: An ancient, traditional story based on supposed historical figures or events. Many legends are based on myths.

MYTH: A story that is not based on historical fact but which uses supernatural characters to explain natural phenomena, such as the weather, seasons, night and day, and so on. Before the scientific facts were known, ancient people used myths to understand the world around them.

ASTRONOMER: Someone who studies space and the heavenly bodies (the stars, planets, moons, etc.).

CALENDAR: A way of recording the year by dividing it into months, weeks, and days, and giving each day a date.

COMPASS: An instrument used in navigation to help people find their way. The points of the compass are north, south, east, and west.

CONSTELLATION: A group of stars that appears to make a distinct pattern in the sky.

DESTINY: The idea that future events in a person's life have already been decided.

NAVIGATION: Finding your way from one place to another, on land, at sea, or in space.

ORBIT: The curved path that one object (such as a planet, moon, or satellite) follows around another object in space.

PHASES: In astronomy, the changing shape of the Moon as it is seen from Earth.

PLANET: One of the heavenly bodies that orbit the Sun, which reflect its light but give out no light of their own. Earth is a planet.

Where's Where

The map below shows where in the world the places named in this book are found.

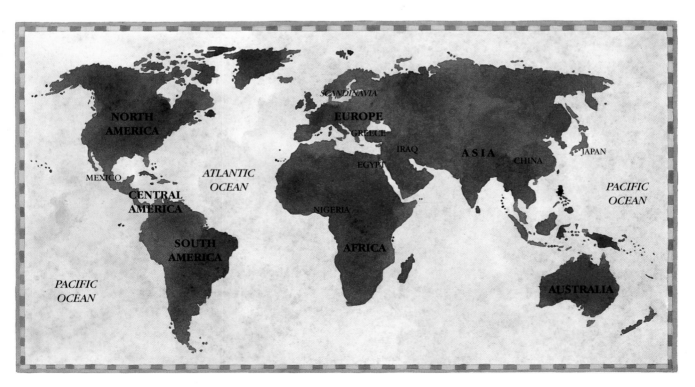

Index